THE BROWN MILE

And Other Rhymes For Motorhoming

Dave Phillips

Foreword

As novices to motorhoming it soon became apparent that every minor disaster that befell us was a rite of passage into a club full of characters you could easily write an epic novel about. I don't have the time nor patience to write an epic novel but I do like a little bit of rhyming verse so here, by popular request, are a few of my observations neatly packaged in Kindle format to save you the weight of carrying a book in your pride and joy.

Some of you know where to find me so if you have any experiences or disasters that arent covered here please let me know and I'll use them to create volume two.

Meanwhile.. enjoy!

Dave

CONTENTS

It's Not How Big It Is
(It's what you do with it)

I envied their van
It was bigger than mine
They had more wheels
And space for more wine

They had three bikes
On a rack on the back
Yet as I took our turn
As the road turned to track

And tucked in our mirrors
Breathed in, held on tight
En route to the spot
Where we'd spend the night

I thought of those folk
With their bikes and their wine
Raised a glass to their van
So much bigger than mine

PUSH IT IN AND TWIST IT

"Push it in and twist it"
Said the chap in socks and sandals
As I wrestled with that pesky EHU
And resigned myself to spend the night
In a MoHo lit by candles
Who was he to tell me what to do?

I gave that man a vacant stare
That wire limp in my wrist
Confused, concerned and somewhat scared
"Just push it in and twist!"

I'd heard about these MoHo folk
With their bowls of fruit and ducks
So swiftly ran back to my van
Tonight he's out of luck

I'll live without the EHU
It must have been the box
My wire just didn't fit with it
As sandals don't...with socks!

THE BROWN MILE

"It's full" she said "the light is on!"
I'd heard that cry before
I suited up with mask and gloves
And headed for the door

I took the key and turned it
Swung the locker open wide
Held my nose, detached the hose
And quickly reached inside

Pulled the handle, gave a tug
And straight on out it came
That plastic box of fragrant sludge
Thetford was its name

And conscious of all eyes on me
I rustled up a smile
And slowly, surely, step by step
Set forth on the Brown Mile.

BATTERY OF LEISURE

I'm a battery of leisure
I linger in your van
I live in the garage or under your seat
They put me where they can

Occasionally, now and then
I'll give you something back
But mostly I just lounge around
Up front, or down the back

Your trickle sunlight into me
I feed when you're plugged in
I'm a battery of leisure
Now please pour me a gin

RUBIKS BED

There's a folding, drop down, lift up bed
In the middle of our van
With twisty, turny, locking bits
That I don't understand

There's a table top that I assume
Needs somewhere else to be
And a jigsaw made of cushions
That's beyond the likes of me

I've read the book from front to back
Yet still don't have a clue
And thus my four berth Motorhome
Sleeps a maximum of two!

THE SCOTTISH PROBLEM

You're adept at solving issues
With the boiler and the fridge
You've solved the bog not flushing
But you cannot solve the midge

You've turned away from narrow lanes
Avoided each low bridge
VOSA haven't pulled you in
But you cannot miss the midge

Your forearms look like join the dots
You've tried citronella and "Smidge"
You've sprayed yourself with DDT
But you'll never be rid of the midge

So before heading North of the border
Be sure that you're wholly prepared
To be eaten alive in short order
Until all that remains is your hair

THE GREYWATER MYSTERY

We'd filled the water to the brim
We'd emptied the grey waste
The Thetford was no longer grim
Of turds there were no trace

We went away for two whole days
We filled the kettle thrice
Between us we'd had seven pees
And one "forced sacrifice"

We'd washed up twice but both those times
The plug had been in place
So please imagine my surprise
When emptying the waste

That water flowed for half an hour
Before it trickled thin
I'm fairly sure that more came out
Than ever we put in

UNCOUPLED

Brenda and Norman were happy
They'd both taken early retirement
She'd worked forty years as a nurse
He'd worked a few less as a fireman

They'd always dreamt they would travel
Now that all of their children had grown
So they scoured the land until they found a grand
Tag axle, six wheeled Motorhome

Norman did most of the driving
Brenda kept everything clean
Except when it came to the Thetford
They seemed to be living the dream

Yet soon their new freedom brought fractures
"How could the satnav be wrong"
"That awning is at the wrong angle"
"That's a Pooh! I can tell by the pong!"

Now Brenda and Norman had always been close
But proximity comes at a cost
The calling of names, apportioning blame
If by chance you should end up quite lost

Or get stuck in the mud for a moment
Or fail to reverse arrow straight
Park on an incline or run out of wine
Watch love turning slowly to hate

Norman's no longer with Brenda

But don't let their story stop you
Work as a team to realise your dream
And don't use the cludgie for poo!

THE WEIGHTING GAME

It's going to be our home from home
We must take all our things
She handed me a three page list
Of what we were to bring

Four chairs, two tables just in case
Inflatable canoe
Fold up camping kitchen
And not one stove but two

Plates and cups and bowls and pans
A microwave and breville
That little twelve volt hoover
That we call the dirty devil

Windbreak, sunshade, parasol
Sunlounger and stool
Jerry can , electric fan
To keep the midges cool

Twenty frozen ready meals
Fourteen crates of wine
Gin and whisky, wine and beer
Plenty ice and lime

Electric bikes strapped to the back
Surfboards on the roof

And suddenly our engine lacks
The grunt to make us move

THE DOG

He's watching us pack from the window
He knows we are going away
His happiness shows
As he presses his nose
On the glass I just cleaned yesterday

He's bounding across the begonias
His feet barely touching the floor
His tail in the air
Then a whine of despair
As his head hits the motorhome door

He sits on the ground looking doleful
His sorrow is too much to bear
With one turn of the key
I fill him with glee
With one bound he leaps onto his chair

And he doesn't mind as I buckle him in
He knows there are good times ahead
New bottoms to sniff and new places to see
And so many pats on the head

And beaches to run on
And things to explore
And strange people handing out treats
But bestest of all
They'll be throwing his ball
And feeding him barbecued meat

EX-TRACTOR FAN

They never had any hard standing
The weatherman promised us dry
So how is it that I'm now standing
Ankle deep trying to tie

A rope through a hoop in a downpour
Whilst a farmer sits dry at the wheel
Of his warm Massey Ferguson tractor
Watching me making a meal

Of this sodding wet miserable towrope
Now up to my armpits in mud
The weatherman promised us sunshine
Never mentioned a biblical flood

So always insist on hard standing
Go somewhere else if you must
And know that that bloke on the telly
By the map isn't someone to trust

They're At It Again

"Wake up" said she
"They're at it again"
I raised my weary head
"Put that flyscreen down
and come back to bed" I said

"Ooh no" said she "It isn't right"
"She sounds like she's in pain!"
"Put the flyscreen down dear"
I uttered once again

"They've no respect for others"
" They're at it all night long"
"If that's the noise you're supposed to make
We've been doing it all wrong!"

"Put the flyscreen down dear
and cover up your ears
before our naughty neighbours
fill your mind with strange ideas"

"It's way too late for that" said she
"Life's for taking risks"
"Please strap me to the bike rack
And spank me with a whisk!"

WORKING FROM MOHO

Today I'll be working from MoHo
With my laptop remotely connected
Via mobile phone I shall work as I roam
Wheresoever 4g is detected

When we catch up on Zoom
I shall try not to laugh
At the background you use to conceal
Your bare office wall
Whilst I keep you enthralled
With my view ever changing, so real

And should I by chance
Be somewhere in France
With my café au lait and croissant
Don't be dismayed
That I'm working this way
For some of us can… and some can't

SAFARI CHEF

The garage door is open
The kitchen is erected
The orange hose is in his hand
And skilfully connected

To the gas point underneath the flap
Ignition is complete
He dons his special cheffing cap
She passes him the meat

He takes a sip of Cotes Du Rhône
And cooks two steaks quite rare
Then summons forth the pizza stone
A margarita's there

The wife and I watch on with awe
As this culinary fella
Finds a pan within his van
And rustles up paella

"We'll need to buy a grill like that"
She muttered in my ear
I told her she needs no more fat
And now I'm sitting here

Patiently in A and E
Not with her in the van
Hungry, cos I've has no tea
And she broke our only pan

TO INFIRMITY
AND BEYOND

We're none of us getting much younger
The end of the road is in sight
Retirement's arrived
And we're gonna drive
Our MoHo straight into the light

We've equipped it to cope with our frailties
With every aid we can afford
There's a rail at the door
To help us off the floor
And assist us in climbing aboard

There are matching mobility scooters
Housed in a trailer we tow
Two walking frames
Embossed with our names
And blue pills for that problem below

It's the sum of our lifetime's endeavours
The realisation of dreams
There's a glass for our teeth
And a fridge underneath
Full of prune juice and haemorrhoid cream

THE SILVER SCREEN

Some folk are seen
On the grand silver screen
Like Bardot, Loren or Monroe
Alas not on mine
Which seems plainly designed
To frustrate me wherever I go

With elastic and straps
The instructions are crap
It's all wrinkled and saggy and torn
It's gonna get binned
Or gone with the wind
A star that should not have been born

I'll buy me some curtains
All velvet and grand
With a rope for the open and closing
You'll find me on stage
In my new golden age
In the pouch I reserve for my posing

THE HABITATION CHECK

With some trepidation
We handed our keys
To an oil stained yet chiselled old bloke
In blue dungarees
With holes in the knees
And fingertips yellowed by smoke

He said " leave her with me"
"I'll take a look see"
"I'll rummage and seek out the damp"
Then he disappeared
Right under the rear
With a screwdriver, ratchet and lamp

I said to the missus
"Let's go get a tea"
"And a scone..whilst we wait for the man"
So we sat with our plates
Having lengthy debate
About cream on the bottom.. or jam

And as time progressed
She became quite distressed
With what the old chap might discover
I said "we'll be fine"
"There's nothing to find"

"Except for our drawer full of rubber!"

My mobile phone buzzed
He said "That's it all done"
"Come on back and I'll show you the list"
Of the damp and the mould
And the pipes that were old
And the other bits easily fixed

>

So we went and we saw
How he'd resealed the door
And dealt with our rat infestation
And seeing us scared
He promptly declared
Her fit for our safe habitation

I pulled out my wallet
And paid the man well
Then let out a triumphant roar
Then looking inside
Saw that drawer open wide
And the contents all over the floor!!

THE RATTLER

From the very first day that we drove her
We've fought an impossible battle
We've used sponges and pads
Now it's not quite so bad
But we can't isolate every rattle

We've wrapped every plate
Place each fork in a sock
Every glass has a box of its own
Shoved everything
In the overhead bins
And filled with expandable foam

Now I sit every morn
Popping pill after pill
To ensure that my day is pain free
And I'm fairly sure
All that's rattling still
Is the cocktail of drugs inside me!

THE TINKERER

If there's a flap he will lift it
He likes buttons and handles and knobs
He's a kid with a toy
An overgrown boy
He'll find work where there isn't a job

He's constantly checking his pressures
He tightens his awning strap twice
He empties the loo
After each number two
He's eager to give folk advice

On how they should level their MoHo
On how they should uncoil their wire
On how they should angle their awning
How often to rotate their tyres

But our motorhome's for relaxing
For sitting and sipping our wine
And watching the tinkerer tinker
As he uses up valuable time

BOARD GAMES

As the rain batters down on the skylight
Or when midges are too much to bear
We open an overhead locker
And thumb through the board games in there

We're fairly proficient at Cluedo
Monopoly stays in its box
Frustration is more fun than Ludo
And Jenga is missing some blocks

We've played Battleships many times over
Mousetrap and Boggle as well
But our favourite game is Welsh Scrabble
Where every letter is L

CAMPSITE CAT

The old campsite cat isn't fussy
The old campsite cat doesn't care
He'll stroll in and curl up on your duvet
And cover your sofas with hair

The campsite cat's fairly well travelled
He's been carried away far and wide
He'll wait til he sees you are leaving
Then deep in your garage he'll hide

Yet somehow despite his adventures
However so far he may roam
His compass seems fairly well centred
And he always finds his way home

So keep an eye out for that rascal
Check every nook in your van
And should you end up with a hitcher
Please take him back when you can

THE FRENCH TRIP

At last we'd reached the moment
The morning had arrived
Two long years off waiting
Now off to France we'd drive

We'd bought the light deflectors
We'd both had all our jabs
We'd take the Channel Tunnel
'Neath the fishes and the crabs

We were full of joie de vivre
It felt great to be alive
Until we hit the traffic
On the old M25

And then the lines of lorries
Heading south on the M2
With its heady scent of rural Kent
And it's roadside portaloos

Wearily we inched out our way
Ever slowly South
And hot and bothered we arrived
At the tunnel's open mouth

And presently we boarded
With no pomp nor circumstance
And forty minutes later
We raised a cheer for France

>

The Douanier just waved us through
We were feeling fairly fine
And headed straight for Carrefour
To fill our van with wine

That night we'd shun the campsite
We'd find some place to park
And watch the sea, my girl and me
And snuggle after dark

So all French and Romantic
We parked upon Le Plage
And woke some time next morning
Twixt a dredger and a barge

Somewhere west of Cap Gris Nez
Where the channel's none too wide
Heading back to Dover
At the mercy of the tide!

TERRY

Terry's out reclining
He's soaking up the rays
He's eyeing up the dolly birds
Like he did in younger days

He's sucking in his tummy
He's flashing them a grin
With the teeth he puts away at night
In a mug above the bin

Terry's turning on the charm
In shorts that match his crocs
He's a motorhoming Romeo
And his van was built to rock

Sheila's washing dishes
Watching Terry watching girls
She knows what Terry wishes
Yet she knows that she's his world

WESTBOUND STORY

We've stocked the van with incense sticks
Our chakra's at is best
There's chanting on the stereo
And our Moho's headed west

We'll pass the Henge and Avebury
And Glastonbury Tor
We'll stop and sip our herbal tea
To cleanse our inner core

We're floating down the three oh three
We're following the line
To the land of myth and magic
And of Buckfast Tonic Wine

A magical elixir
Made by Benedictine monks
Who bear responsibility
For all Glaswegian drunks

NEVILLE WENT DOWN TO HALFORDS

Neville went down to Halfords
He was looking for a bike
A foldy-up electric job
Is what he thought he'd like

The salesman pounced on Neville
Looked him squarely in the eye
"We"ve foldy-up electric jobs
Aplenty for to try!"

"But bicycles that fold in three
take patience and a knack
and my dear man, I see your van
Has a rack upon the back"

Now Neville eyed the salesman
And here's what Neville said
"That rack takes a knack and strength I lack
to lift bikes above my head"

"So kindly show me what you have
in your foldy-electrical section"
And the salesman complied
Neville let out a sigh
At the sight of the salesman's selection

"I'm a man," Neville said
"and won't be seen dead
on a bike lacking crossbar or gears
these feminine shoppers
are nought like the Chopper
I've ridden for many a year"

>

Neville went down to Halfords
He left without a bike
Yet retuned to the van with a bagful
Of other stuff he liked

Batteries and socket sets
And other "manly" trinkets
For no matter how manly a folding bike
Dear Neville doesn't think it

STEALTH VAN

"It's a stealth van" said the owner
"It's just a van" I said
For, to me, it seemed to be
A Transit with a bed

It wasn't very fancy
Nor over engineered
A broken mattress in the back
And a cool bag for his beer

"It's a stealth van" said the owner
In a tone approaching pride
"And if you don't believe me
I'll take you for a ride"

So I belted up beside him
And we exited the field
Headed for the bypass
Where all would be revealed

And there, ahead, a radar trap
And a camera, on a bridge
He said "I have no proper bed
and a cool bag for a fridge

but this old vans a stealth van
although you may think it ain't
and my mates in the Air Force
and he helped me out with paint"

>

I looked down at the speedo
We were pushing ninety four
As we hurtled past the boys in blue
Pedal to the floor

I waited for the sirens
The inevitable lights
And when those sirens never came
I knew that he was right

It really is a Stealth Van
Do not think it ain't
And that young man's now my best pal
And he's getting me some paint

THE INVERTER

"Don't touch that!"I warned her
"You don't know what it does"
"Oh don't be daft" she said to me
"You do make such a fuss"

"It has a little switch on it
It says that it inverts
I'm gonna press that little switch
It surely cannot hurt"

I dived into the captain's chair
And casually clunk-clicked
Grateful for my seatbelt
As upside down we flipped

Now everything not nailed down
Is sitting on the ceiling
We're totally inverted
And I've got a funny feeling

She'll listen to me next time
When I warn her not to fiddle
For our inverter's in the bathroom
And her hair's now soaked with piddle

MR (OR MRS) FIX IT

Whenever you're in trouble
Whenever leaks appear
When the boilers kaput or the garage won't shut
When the fridge begins warming you beer

I'll guarantee that really quite near
There's a man or a woman who knows
They'll reach into their van and swift reappear
With a grommet, a bolt or a hose

They'll know all about oscillation
And sine waves and blow, bang and suck
They'll know what to do when you can't flush the loo
And when to use gaffer or duck

They're the well equipped MoHo messiah
The font of all knowledge of vans
There's nought they don't know
And they're where you should go
Whenever the Pooh hits the fan*

*if it does this you are upside down.. please see "The Inverter"

THE INCIDENT

I'm keeping a fair distance
The firemen are here
I'm waiting on the signal
To tell us it's all clear

I'd just been in the cludgie
She'd given me abuse
I couldn't really help it
My insides were quite loose

From an overdose of sweeties
I knew that I'd done wrong
But I love the noise that space dust makes
As it crackles on my tongue

And the atmosphere grew frosty
After that which I had done
I'd broken Thetford's golden rule
"It's just for number ones"

She'd asked the folk on websites
For advise on how to clean it
She'd sent them photos on her phone
And everyone who'd seen it

Told her buy the cheapest cola
And pour it down the pan
And so she did and that is why
I'm stood outside my van

For there'd been a great explosion

That had blown us off our feet
For Aldi Cola doesn't mix
With popping candy sweets

THAT SINKING FEELING

The Commodore's a tidy sort of fellow
All his things are diligently stowed
Hoses and cables
All ship shape and labelled
In lockers he refers to as "The Hold"

He's never ever seen without a tie on
He's always very elegantly dressed
And there's one thing that I'm sure you can rely on
His van contains a Corby trouser press

His shoes are highly polished and as shiny
As the mischievous wee twinkle in his eye
As he tells of his adventures on the briny
He walks with shoulders back and head held high

Shirley is his trophy, she's much younger
She's brassy, busty, blonde and bouncy too
She cooks and cleans and satisfies his hunger
And does whatever he commands her too

The Commodore talks loudly of his conquests
Of how he once had girls in every port
How Shirley is the one he's "owned" the longest
As she sits there in the clothes that she's been bought

The Commodore thinks that he is respected
He's sure that he's a cut above the rest

And the pretty souvenir that he has collected
Is bound to leave us other folk impressed

His motor home's a bloody huge Rapido
A super yacht consigned unto the land
And I'm hoping sometime soon it gets torpedoed
And Shirley finds a more deserving man

"Wood Burning Stove"

The van next to ours is a Commer
It belongs in a transport museum
It's owners have been here all summer
To be honest it's quite rare to see 'em

His hair flows on down to his ankles
His stare always vacant and calm
Her dress sense is pure vintage Woodstock
She has peace signs tattooed on her arm

Their van has a cast iron chimney
It smokes every day and all night
Churning out fog which relaxes our dog
And makes everything seem alright

They're at one with the universe baby
They gave me a bracelet they wove
And I'm heading over there maybe
To sit by their "wood burning stove"

IDLE HANDS

It's said the devil will find work
For idle hands to do
My devil makes me deal with waste
And empty out the loo

She makes me put the awning up
She makes me make her tea
Then makes me make another cup
And tune in the TV

And should I try to take a seat
Should I feel fit to drop
She'll notice we've run out of sweets
And send me to the shop

But worry not about me chum
I'm sure I will be fine
For I've been slipping Valium
Into my devil's wine

RUSSIAN ROULETTE

There's a road at the top of Loch Lomond
A "low road" as mentioned in song
It has only two lanes
It's no fun in the rain
And things don't take much to go wrong

You could end up in very deep water
You could quickly collide with a cliff
And on either edge
There's a bit of a ledge
That could easily send you skew-wiff

So most folk keep off of the verges
But that's not the best thing to do
As from each bend a vehicle emerges
That's doing the same thing as you

And at that point if you'll keep your mirror
Depends on that oncoming threat
The best thing by far
Is a very small car
But really it's Russian Roulette

ALL THE BEST TUNES

The Devil has all the best tunes
And I feel obliged to let her
Play them in our Motorhome
Although my stuff would be better

We're kids who were born in the sixties
So the eighties is when we went dancing
My memories of the school discos
We're disco and punk and romancing

Whereas her teenage years seem quite different
There was Elvis and Country and Western
And at her school dance there was little romance
And her grandmother's record collection

Neil Diamond and ABBA and old Johnny Cash
Are the things that she listens to still
And should I insist on playing "The Smiths"
She gives me a look that could kill

But the devil does all of the driving
And I'm bound to do all that it takes
To allow her to choose, to keep her amused
And ensure that she stays wide awake!

THE OWNERS CLUB

"Ooh look" said Jane
"Their van's the same
Model as ours only newer"
"Let's go say hello
They might give us a go
Or at very least let us look through her"

I let out a sigh
Started wondering why
We needed to seek out our own
Why we needed to stick
To our own little clique
And leave other owners alone

Why like birds of a feather
Owners clubs meet
To commune, to contrast and compare
When I like my picture
Wide and complete
And I'm perfectly happy to share

Stories and knowledge and, if I must, wine
With whoever I happen to meet
And should your van happen
To be quite unlike mine
Rest assured I'm not here to compete!

MONSTER FROM THE BROWN LAGOON

We'd laid our weary heads to sleep
The blinds had all been drawn
There'd been no need for counting sheep
We'd slumber til the morn

Or so I thought 'til half past two
When she shook me from my slumber
She said "there's noises from the loo!"
I said "what am I… a plumber?"

But as I opened up my ears
I heard that she was right
There was something in our waterworks
Making noises in the night

I said "get up and take a look"
She hit me round the head
Which was a hint I quickly took
To take a look instead

I grabbed a mallet from the shelf
It's handy it was there
Took a dram to steel myself
Got myself prepared

Then eased the bathroom door ajar
And peered into the pan

I saw a sight that wasn't right
In any kind of van

>

A brown and slimy tentacle
Protruded from the lip
I whacked it with my mallet
And down the hole it slipped

And here I stand, I have it trapped
Within this here cassette
I hear it writhing in the crap
I might keep it as a pet

And take it on the road with us
As we journey site to site
And bring it out from time to time
To give you all a fright

THE BOG
WHISPERER

Should your pipe work not be clearing
Should your red light not go out
If your pee keeps reappearing
It's time to give a shout

To that man on every campsite
Who knows just what to do
The King of all things Khazi
The Shaman of the loo

He'll listen to your lavatory
He'll quickly understand
He'll speak in tongue then deftly plunge
Wrist deep with his right hand

And before you've time to give him thanks
He'll swiftly disappear
For there's other folk with pipes and tanks
For the whisperer to clear

WEIGHT WATCHERS

The bits and bobs were loaded
The comfy chairs and table
Down below we'd neatly stowed
The hoses and the cables

And now at last the time was here
'Twas time to cross that bridge
To calculate the space for beer
And food within our fridge

Five hundred grams per ready meal
Would swiftly escalate
And the axles joined unto our wheels
Could soon be overweight

So we've come to a decision
That Cup-a-soups are fine
And we'll only keep the fridge on
For Prosecco, Beer and wine

You may come to an assumption
That my ratios are wrong
But by process of consumption
That fridge ain't full for long!

DAMPER CAMPERS

'Twas a rain licked Summer evening
The showers just wouldn't relent
We watched from the dry
As our young neighbours tried
To put up a minuscule tent

The wind gathered pace and I saw on the face
Of those campers a look of despair
A miserable frown
As the hail belted down
And settled right back in my chair

My wife looked at me and I looked at my wife
She knew well that I couldn't resist
Inviting them in
For a warm and some gin
And gradually help them get (drunk}

Enough to not care
That the weather out there
Would soak through their tent like a sieve
But now they'll understand
That to camp in a van
Is the warmest and best way to live

THINGS THAT GO WRONG IN THE NIGHT

It seems that there's a gremlin
Running riot as we sleep
He waits until the van is dark
Then into it he creeps

He'll disable all your sockets
He'll bung up all your plumbing
Til the flush comes up to meet you
At the hole you put your bum in

He'll fiddle with the boiler
He'll nibble on a knob
He'll tinker with the fuse box
To ensure that there's a job

To deal with in the morning
Once you're chairs are safely stowed
And you've rolled away your awning
Just before you hit the road

That's when you'll discover
What the little blighters done
One thing or another
To stop you having fun

But stop and count your blessings
You'll soon be on your way
And pray he's not been messing
Within your engine bay

HIGHLAND RETREAT

There's an art to highland driving
On the narrowest of lanes
In a landscape unforgiving
Where it more than often rains

You'll learn who has the right of way
Who takes the passing place
And learn who has the final say
When you come face to face

With sixty tons of timber
Bound for sunny Inverness
At fifty miles an hour
You'll understand distress

As you fumble quickly for reverse
And make a swift retreat
Unsure which deviation's worse
The water… or the peat

And once the monster's roared on by
And you've been and changed your pants
You'll gaze out on the misty moors
The beautiful expanse

Of Scotland's Northern wastelands
Where the bagpipes ring aloud
And then you'll find your road ahead
Is blocked by Highland cows

>

Who stand their proudly three abreast
You'll feel those nervous twinges
As they stand stubborn, unimpressed
Staring through their fringes

You'll look at them
They'll look at you
They'll fart and resolutely chew
You have a horn but they have two
They'll pave the road with tartan poo
And you'll know what you need to do..

Run Away!

LAND OF THE FLIES

"There's a fly in here"
She said to me
"There's more than one"
Said I
"But we've had all the flyscreens shut!"
Came her quite perturbed reply

"They must have muscled in en masse
When we first opened the door
To pop out and turn on the gas
Once we'd parked up by the shore"

We counted twenty two in all
Some airborne and some not
And fly spray seemed the only tin
Of stuff we hadn't got

I vowed to murder every one
And send their souls to hell
But rolled up magazines and plastic windows
Don't go well

"Swat!" She cried and "No!" Cried I
"I'm not prepared to risk it!"
"Surely we could round them up
And make Garibaldi biscuits?"

THE SOLOIST

The soloist shuns conversation
He carries his life in his van
He sits with a straight poker face on
He cooks all his meals in one pan

The soloist parks in the corner
Moves on every couple of days
He's not one for making acquaintance
He's adept at diverting his gaze

The soloist's never seen drinking
His blinds are drawn just after tea
Who knows what the soloist's thinking
Or what his back story may be

The soloist may be a killer
Maybe I'm being unfair
But I'd love to peek inside his chiller
To see what he's hiding in there

CRISIS... WHAT CRISIS?

Debbie's daily driver
Was a one point three Fiesta
Then her hubby bought a motorhome
As if, she thought, to test her

Now Debbie's not the kind of girl
Who's gives on to her fear
So, soon, she leapt into the cab
Grabbed the wheel, engaged first gear

Which resulted in catastrophe
Things couldn't be much worse
They'd still have a garage
If she had found reverse

As time progressed her confidence
Bent pillars and bent posts
And there's many a dented garden fence
On the roads around the coast

And now she's had a letter
From the government to thank her
For her recent application
To drive a petrol tanker

OCTOBER

Not a cloud was in the sky
The moon was full and bright
Stars twinkled in the heavens
As we parked up for the night

In a campsite near Caernarfon
Twixt the mountains and the sea
The missus stuck the kettle on
We had a cup of tea

We'd come away for Halloween
To escape the Trick or Treaters
There came a knock upon the door
'Twas the owner, keen to meet us

He told us where the grey waste went
He pointed out the loo
He said that he'd much rather
We used green liquid., than blue

And then he bade us a goodnight
And walked away apace
A knowing twinkle in his eye
A smile upon his face

We both slept well and in in the morn
Birdsong filled the air
Hearts full of joy we watched the dawn
And laughed without a care

The owner was a kindly soul
There was fresh bread at our door
He'd left the morning paper
Who could wish for any more?

The headlines told an awful tale
Of a camper and a bus
Two souls released to haunt North Wales
And those two souls.... are us!!

Printed in Great Britain
by Amazon

68602626R00037